G
→ *Video Experience* ←

TONY EVANS
KINGDOM
SINGLE

LIVING COMPLETE AND
FULLY FREE

TYNDALE HOUSE PUBLISHERS, INC.
CAROL STREAM, ILLINOIS

FOCUS ON THE FAMILY®

Kingdom Single Group Video Experience Participant's Guide
© 2019 Focus on the Family. All rights reserved.

Based on the book *Kingdom Single* by Dr. Tony Evans, © 2018 Tony Evans. Published by Tyndale House Publishers, Inc., and Focus on the Family

A Focus on the Family book published by Tyndale House Publishers, Carol Stream, Illinois 60188

For information about special discounts for bulk purchases, please contact Tyndale House Publishers at csresponse@tyndale.com, or call 1-800-323-9400.

ISBN 978-1-58997-983-3

Printed in the United States of America

25   24   23   22
7   6   5   4   3   2

Contents

Welcome, Kingdom Singles!

Walking in the way of a kingdom single is refreshing and empowering. These aren't always the terms used for singles, we know. But beginning now, singles can discover their true spiritual freedom through this dynamic course.

At the core of each session in this course is a video presentation featuring Dr. Tony Evans, author of *Kingdom Single*. Dr. Evans' inspired teaching will give singles new insights into biblical principles as well as assurances that God has a purpose for each and every kingdom single.

To make these truths come alive, you'll find these sections in each session:

The Gathering
Read this brief excerpt to focus on the subject at hand. Answer the questions that follow the passage. If you run out of time, finish the section at home.

Show Time!
Use this section as you view and think about the DVD presentation; it includes thought-provoking questions and biblical input.

Transformation Moments
This brief wrap-up will help you find encouragement and ideas for applying the teaching to your own life.

Note: The DVD presentations and this guide are intended as general advice only, and are not meant to replace clinical counseling, medical treatment, legal counsel, or pastoral guidance.

Focus on the Family maintains a referral network of Christian counselors. For information, call 1-855-771-HELP (4357) or contact www.FocusontheFamily.com/counseling.

1

◊ ◊ ◊

COMPLETE AND FULLY FREE

The Main Point

Kingdom singles are already complete and able to fully maximize that completeness by willingly placing themselves under the rule of God and living within His boundaries of freedom.

The Gathering

To find out more about the kingdom single's completeness, read the following excerpt from *Kingdom Single*. If you have time, answer the questions that appear at the end of the selection. Or you can finish the section at home.

 ## HE COMPLETES YOU

If you're looking for a romantic partner to complete you as a kingdom single, you really don't understand what Jesus Christ has already done.

Because in Him, you are as complete as complete comes. Now, you may not realize that truth. You may not identify with that truth. And if you don't, you're not living out the full benefits of that truth. But none of those things makes the truth any less true. Colossians 2:10 tells us, "In Him you have been made complete, and He is the head over all rule and authority." To think otherwise is to make the institution of marriage, and your desire for a marriage partner, an idol. And idolatry is sin.

Friend, Jesus Christ completes you. That's the truth. Thus, what a romantic partner can provide must remain outside of that, in addition to it, or alongside it. He or she cannot complete you because Jesus already has. If you are not aware or mindful of this reality, there's a danger that you will be expecting too much of another human being, asking him or her to be or do something that only God Himself can be and do.

Far too often, we try to transfer what we see in movies to our real lives. But that places pressure on us and the other people in our lives to live up to a standard we were never designed to fulfill.

As you grow in your understanding, discovery, and acceptance of your completeness in Jesus Christ, you will experience the victory, authority, and intimacy He has already secured for you in Him. You will then be freed up to experience other relationships at a level they were designed for. . . .

Relational issues arise when the focus of either person (or both) shifts from God to each other as the deciding factor, influencer, or even source of completion. That's exactly what happened in the Garden of Eden, after all, which led to the Fall.

Only when you understand and embrace the truth that Christ Himself completes you will you be able to view any current or potential relationship for what it can actually provide—a companion to come alongside you. You'll be amazed at how fulfilling and satisfying a relationship can be when expectations are normalized, the benefit of the doubt (coupled with grace) becomes natural, and you both look to God to lead, fill, satisfy, and complete you.[1]

If someone were to ask you to define "being single," what would you say? In what ways has our culture influenced your definition of singleness? Why does singleness seem to be a negative to many people? Why do so many single Christians consider themselves incomplete?

Show Time!

In session 1 of the *Kingdom Single Group Video Experience*, Dr. Tony Evans lays out the first principle in our study: As a kingdom single, you are already complete.

◊ ◊ ◊

After viewing Tony Evans' presentation "Complete and Fully Free," use the following questions to help you think through what you saw and heard.

1. Dr. Evans referred to Colossians 2:10 to emphasize our completeness in Christ: "In Him you have been made complete, and He is the head over all rule and authority." What does it mean to be complete in Christ?

   Describe the connection between completeness in Christ and alignment under His rule.

What consequences could Christians face when they choose to make decisions outside of His overarching rule?

2. Dr. Evans said that as long as you continue to view yourself as "incomplete" as a single, you will cause yourself to constantly focus on what you lack—rather than on all you have. Describe what can happen when two "incomplete" people wind up together in a dating or marriage relationship.

Tony Evans said that one reason many marriages break up is that there are too many singles getting married who didn't first learn what it means to be "completely single." What does it mean to be "completely single"?

3. Which of the following areas have caused you to feel the most "incomplete" as a single? Check the boxes that apply or write in your own.

- ☐ financial freedom
- ☐ lack of pure sexual engagement
- ☐ social life
- ☐ church events or church groups organized by marital status
- ☐ life chores (fixing things, mowing the lawn, etc.)
- ☐ companionship needs
- ☐ conversations about marriage or spouses
- ☐ household responsibilities handled yourself
- ☐ vacations
- ☐ long-term planning
- ☐ attending events (even at church) or dining alone
- ☐ movies, songs, or other forms of entertainment that emphasize couples
- ☐ other _____
- ☐ other _____
- ☐ other _____

While each of these areas can prove to be a challenge, God promises to supply your every need when you look to Him. Have you ever experienced God's provision in any of the areas listed above through someone other than a spouse? Describe that experience.

Do you thank God for meeting your needs as a single even when He does so in unconventional ways, or do you take it for granted? Explain your answer.

4. Dr. Evans shared Adam's call to "cultivate" the Garden (Genesis 2:15). He used this as an example of freely maximizing your life (time, talents, and treasures) within the context of relationship with God. In what ways was Adam's life in the Garden a life of freedom?

God gave Adam one restriction: He must not eat from the tree of the knowledge of good and evil. According to Dr. Evans, how did that restriction affect Adam's freedom?

What "garden" has God given you to "cultivate"? Are you fully faithful in doing so or are there ways you can do more?

5. List some of the things singles often tell themselves that keep them from freely engaging their time, talents, and treasures for the purposes of God.

Have you ever fallen prey to any of these thoughts? Describe the result.

6. Dr. Evans says that kingdom singles are unmarried believers who have committed themselves to fully and freely maximizing their completeness under the rule of God. Look at the following list and check the boxes of some of the ways a person can maximize his or her completeness. Also write in your own responses.

- ☐ traveling
- ☐ binge-watching Netflix
- ☐ shopping
- ☐ taking personal development courses
- ☐ volunteering to help the disadvantaged
- ☐ learning new skills
- ☐ studying Scripture
- ☐ sulking
- ☐ browsing on social media for extended periods of time
- ☐ praying and meditating
- ☐ socializing
- ☐ teaching Sunday school
- ☐ receiving career development training
- ☐ other _____
- ☐ other _____
- ☐ other _____

Explain why you checked some boxes and left other boxes unchecked.

7. What would change in your life—at your work, with

your immediate or extended family, or in your circle of influence—if you committed yourself to maximizing your freedom within the boundaries of Christ's overarching rule?

8. Read the following excerpt from *Kingdom Single* and reflect on the questions at the end.

HE COMPLETES YOU

Far too many couples are married and yet still feel alone because they never fully knew what it meant to be fully single. So they are grasping for something both in and from their spouse that their spouse often lacks the capacity to provide. The nature of marriage is not merely what you're *getting from* someone else, but also what you're *giving to* someone else. And what you should be giving your spouse is a completely whole single Christian, not half of one who is incomplete.

Friend, you are not fully ready to be married until you're a fully functioning kingdom single. Otherwise, like most people, all you're doing is bringing your incompleteness into a relationship, expecting that relationship to accomplish what it is unable to do. All the marriage will do is reveal that you never fully learned what it meant to be single. To put it succinctly, you are complete in Christ with or without marriage. . . .

Imagine the strain and drain a relationship suffers when one or both people look to the other as their source of completion. Modern psychiatry might call that codependency, not love. Keep in mind, no human being is equipped to offer you what it cost the God of the universe—His own Son's life—to both win and secure. So the first step in living with a kingdom mind-set is understanding that by Christ's sitting next to the Father on the throne, Christ has declared both His ability and His right to complete you.

What does it mean to live as a complete single?

Our English word *single* comes from the joining of the Latin word *singulus* and the Old French word *simplus*. Together, they become more than what most people understand the cultural, contemporary term *single* to mean. Rather than "alone," "unattached," "unmarried," or "by oneself," a more literal translation of these two original words would be "simply unique" or "uniquely simple." Both of those better illustrate the biblical concept of singleness. Other defining terms attached to the original words are "singular," "complete," and "whole."

God never established singleness to be a burdensome, lonesome, pointless, and frustrating existence, as so many have falsely labeled it today. Rather, it is the very "simplicity" of the single life (which we will go into more deeply in Scripture later) that frees a person to fully live out his or her own "uniqueness" and "completeness."

Singleness positions people to become their best version of themselves as no other relational role can. God does not want singles to look to marriage as a way to stop being *single*. People are always to maintain their wholeness, completeness, and uniqueness as individuals, even (and especially) when they get married. . . .

The apostle Paul personally understood the strengths and successes of the single lifestyle far better than do the social commentators of our day. His inspired words in the New Testament present us with a challenge that cuts across the grain of our society. According to Paul:

Being single is a very good thing (see 1 Corinthians 7:26).

Yes, there's a good deal of controversy surrounding that concept, even though it's every bit as biblical as John 3:16. But make no mistake about what Paul is saying: *If you are single, you're in the best possible spiritual position.*

Now, this may be contrary to what you've heard about singleness or even what you feel about it, but God's Word often runs contrary to popular opinion. God never set out to be popular. He set out to be God. And God says it is highly beneficial for a person to be single. God is not opposed to marriage; He created it, and it has its own purposes. But when comparing the two for which state allows for the understanding and fulfilling of one's purpose, being single wins.

Whether you want to be single or married, let that truth sink in for a moment. Let the high value God places on your status assure you that your life is not a mistake and this season does not have to be disappointing.

Singleness is not a second-class status. It's not to be a perpetual waiting period. Singleness is a unique platform and position provided to you for great enjoyment, accomplishment, discovery, exploration, freedom, and meaning. To not maximize your season of singleness because you're so focused on waiting for marriage or disappointed in the present is to waste your God-given gift. Never miss out on today's open doors for those you are hoping will open tomorrow.[2]

What strategies does Satan use to negatively affect your concept of being single? In what way does even the Christian culture contribute to these attacks? First Corinthians 7:26 calls singleness a very good thing. Describe some "very good" aspects of the single life both from a biblical standpoint and also from a contemporary standpoint.

Transformation Moments
Read the following passage from the book of Ephesians. Answer

the questions that follow. If you run out of time, finish this section at home.

But God, being rich in mercy, because of His great love with which He loved us, even when we were dead in our transgressions, made us alive together with Christ (by grace you have been saved), and raised us up with Him, and seated us with Him in the heavenly places in Christ Jesus, so that in the ages to come He might show the surpassing riches of His grace in kindness toward us in Christ Jesus. For by grace you have been saved through faith; and that not of yourselves, it is the gift of God; not as a result of works, so that no one may boast. For we are His workmanship, created in Christ Jesus for good works, which God prepared beforehand so that we would walk in them.

EPHESIANS 2:4-10

The phrase "surpassing riches of His grace in kindness toward us" describes God's heart toward you. In what ways, as a single, has God shown you kindness? In what ways can singleness give you the freedom to do more good works for the kingdom than if you were married? Are you maximizing these moments or wasting them in a "spirit of waiting"? What can you do this week to maximize your status of singleness for God's kingdom?

2

◊ ◊ ◊

CALLED FOR
A PURPOSE

The Main Point

A kingdom single has a specific assignment, or calling, to oversee and fulfill.

The Gathering

To find out more about fulfilling your calling as a single Christian, read the following excerpt from *Kingdom Single*. If you have time, answer the questions that appear at the end of the selection. Or you can finish the section at home.

 ## YOUR PURPOSE

As a single, it's critical to identify and live out your purpose. This is such a free season for you to explore your gifts, passions, and experiences and how they merge into your calling. Don't let other people or your own feelings of disappointment distract you from passionately pursuing your calling. Remember, the quickest way for God to get you where He wants you is for Him to be able to use you where He has you. . . .

You have been uniquely created by God for the special purpose He has for you to use for His glory, your good, and the help of others. A kingdom calling will fulfill you and benefit those around you while highlighting God and His power, grace, and mercy.

You may know your calling now, or you may simply know bits and pieces of it. Whatever it is you do know, I want to encourage you to get busy doing that. God always hits a moving target. What was Adam doing when he found a wife? He wasn't out girl watching, because there were no other human beings around. He wasn't daydreaming about his wedding day. Adam was busy functioning in his God-given role of tending the Garden of Eden and, more specifically, naming the animals.

Likewise, God doesn't want you sitting around, so focused on your wedding day that you miss out on the pleasures and purpose He has for you today. He wants you functioning for Him until, or even if, He creates your wedding day. He wants you fully thriving in your purpose right now. . . .

Living freely and fully for Christ in your calling as an unmarried believer will require a change of your focus—from preoccupation with marriage, your past, future, lack, or desires to a preoccupation with Jesus and His purpose for your life. Paul wrote in 1 Corinthians 7:35, "This I say for your own benefit; not to put a restraint upon you, but to promote what is appropriate and to secure undistracted devotion to the Lord." . . .

Paul was not trying to handcuff single Christians and keep the two sexes apart in what he wrote. He wasn't trying to prevent people from desiring to get married or pursuing matrimony. He wasn't anti-marriage at all. But there's a benefit in being single that Paul wanted to make sure his readers understood as well. This benefit is "undistracted devotion to the Lord." One way Satan robs us of God's best is to cause a disturbance in our lives to distract us, much the way one thief may distract a store clerk so the other thief can steal merchandise or money without being noticed.[1]

How does pursuing God's purpose for your life affect you, others, and the kingdom of God? What advantage does the single Christian have in pursuing God's calling for his or her life? What are some common distractions that married couples might face that could take away from their focus on God? In what ways are you maximizing this season of undistracted devotion to God?

Show Time!

In session 2 of the *Kingdom Single Group Video Experience*, Dr. Evans lays out the second principle in our study: Every kingdom single has a specific assignment, or calling, to oversee and fulfill.

◊ ◊ ◊

After viewing Tony Evans' presentation "Called for a Purpose," use the following questions to help you think through what you saw and heard.

1. Dr. Evans recalls the experience of going on Sunday drives and compares it to the aimlessness of many single Christians. What do you think causes many single Christians to be aimless?

    Why is an aimless life ultimately unfulfilling for Christians? Contrast this with a life lived pursuing God's purpose.

2. Dr. Evans told about a living mannequin he and his wife, Lois, observed in New York. Many sought to distract her

from her work. What are some common distractions Satan uses to shift the focus of a single person away from God?

Distractions are not always bad things. They may be good things that simply aren't to be *your* things. Can you identify some "good" distractions that are common to our culture?

The living mannequin was committed to her work and refused to be distracted. How can you limit distractions so that you can be more committed to living out your purpose?

3. Think of someone you know who is living out his or her purpose with devotion and passion. Describe what you observe about this person's life. What lessons can you learn from this example?

4. Dr. Evans says that your calling consists of a combination of your gifts, passions, experiences, intersections, vision, and personality. Knowing your passions is a great place to start. Check the boxes that interest you and write in other interests that aren't listed.

   ☐ helping others
   ☐ being a listening ear
   ☐ creating charts and graphs
   ☐ analyzing and strategizing
   ☐ exploring the arts (music, theater, writing)
   ☐ teaching others
   ☐ giving to others (money, material items)
   ☐ following politics
   ☐ working toward personal reform
   ☐ studying
   ☐ meditating
   ☐ socializing
   ☐ seeking social reform
   ☐ fighting for justice
   ☐ desiring racial reconciliation
   ☐ other _____
   ☐ other _____

Summarize how your interests converge to create an overarching umbrella of passion.

5. Spiritual gifts are often confused with interests and skills. However, spiritual gifts are special gifts from the Holy Spirit that help you experience and expand God's presence in the world around you. Most people have more than one spiritual gift. Check the boxes of the gifts you have noticed in yourself or that others have noticed in you.

- ☐ mercy
- ☐ leadership
- ☐ administration
- ☐ wisdom
- ☐ prophecy
- ☐ faith
- ☐ giving
- ☐ hospitality
- ☐ service
- ☐ missions
- ☐ teaching

- ☐ preaching/podcasting
- ☐ evangelism
- ☐ discernment
- ☐ encouragement
- ☐ helps
- ☐ knowledge
- ☐ other _____
- ☐ other _____

In what ways are you seeking to develop the spiritual gifts you have been given?

6. We have looked at passions and gifts, but there are other areas of life the Lord uses in establishing your personal purpose. Briefly define each one (descriptions of these can be found on pages 30–31 of *Kingdom Single*):

Experiences:

Intersections:

Vision:

Personality:

7. Dr. Evans says, "When all six of those elements come together, you will begin to experience what it is to be undivided and focused in your purpose." Reflect on these six areas in your own life. Take notes here to help you discern your calling and purpose.

Passions:

Gifts:

Experiences:

Intersections:

Vision:

Personality:

8. What conclusions can you draw about what God is calling you to do? In what ways are you already fulfilling your calling?

Do you need to understand everything about your calling before you begin pursuing it? Why or why not?

9. Read the following excerpt from *Kingdom Single* and reflect on the questions at the end.

 ## DIVISION AND DISTRACTION

In bowling, every lane is occupied by a single bowler. That bowler's total focus needs to be on the impact he or she can make. The moment that bowler starts noticing what's happening with other bowlers on other lanes, he will mess up his own ability to have his own impact, or she may even wind up rolling gutter balls.

I understand that in our world of social media consumption, comparisons happen daily, if not hourly. But the measurement of your life as a single is not to be compared with other singles, or even married couples. God has a purpose for you, and it won't line up with His purpose for others. Seize the days you have as a single, and avoid the temptation of distraction through comparison during this season of your life.

Satan uses comparison to disturb so many Christian singles and worry them about their marital status or being "incomplete" that he's running amok through their lives, stealing their joy and robbing them of their effectiveness for Christ. When your focus shifts from Christ to yourself, a thief is at work on you, seeking to rob you of your sense of completeness as a kingdom single.

Paul's point in 1 Corinthians 7 is that married people, by virtue of being married, are divided. They have divided responsibilities. They need to please their spouse, fulfill their purpose, and please God. They're constantly shifting among different focuses, because the very nature of the relationships forces the division.

But a Christian single is undivided.

So many singles today are frustrated, however, because they're experiencing as a single what they should be experiencing only if they were married: They're divided. By being consumed with thoughts about marriage, dating, finding a mate, and sex, they're living under the strain of divided responsibilities. If God hasn't given you a mate to worry about yet, leave that person alone in your priorities, time, and thoughts. Because that person doesn't exist yet. Keep the desire, lose the distraction.

I advise singles who are struggling with the overwhelming desire for marriage to take one meal or day a week to fast and pray about their desire. Then don't revisit the issue until the following week. This way they are spiritually addressing the issue without being consumed by it.

The moment you're divided emotionally and spiritually, you have let your singleness get in the way of God's kingdom calling for your life and well-being. If you're spending an inordinate amount of time thinking about marriage, looking at wedding dresses, watching television programs about people getting married or being married, dating person after person, or scrolling through screens of prospects online, and as a result you're feeling frustrated and distracted, you have been pulled away from a spiritual focus.

A successful kingdom single is one who seeks to maximize his or her singleness for the betterment of self and others, the advancement of God's kingdom, and the manifestation of His glory.

Here's the question every single should ask: "God, how do You want me to use the state I'm in until You change my state for Your maximum purpose?"[2]

Why is comparison so dangerous to the Christian single? What tempts the single Christian to divide his or her focus on God's calling? What boundaries could you place in your life to keep your focus on God's calling? Consider the question Dr. Evans asks in the last sentence of the excerpt above. How do you think God would answer that question if you were to ask Him today? Pray and ask God to give you wisdom and insight.

Transformation Moments

Read the following passage from the book of 1 Corinthians. Answer the questions that follow. If you run out of time, finish this section at home.

Now concerning virgins I have no command of the Lord, but I give an opinion as one who by the mercy of the Lord is trustworthy. I think then that this is good in view of the present distress, that it is good for a man to remain as he is. Are you bound to a wife? Do not seek to be released. Are you released from a wife? Do not seek a wife. But if you marry, you have not sinned; and if a virgin marries, she has not sinned. Yet such will have trouble in this life, and I am trying to spare you. But this I say, brethren, the time has been shortened, so that from now on those who have wives should be as though they had none; and those who weep, as though they did not weep; and those who rejoice, as though they did not rejoice; and those who buy, as though they did not possess; and those who use the world, as though they did not make full use of it; for the form of this world is passing away.

But I want you to be free from concern. One who is unmarried is concerned about the things of the Lord, how he may please the Lord; but one who is married is concerned about the things of the world, how he may please his wife, and his interests are divided. The woman who is unmarried, and the virgin, is concerned about the things of the Lord, that she may be holy both in body and spirit; but one who is married is concerned about the things of the world, how she may please her husband. This I say for your own benefit; not to put a restraint upon you, but to promote what is appropriate and to secure undistracted devotion to the Lord.

I CORINTHIANS 7:25-35

Paul says that he wants his readers to be free from the concerns of marriage. What are some realities of marriage that Paul may be referring to? In the next sentence, Paul uses the word *concern* in a different sense. Describe the differences between the two types of concern in this passage. How could the phrase "concerned about the things of the Lord" be explained in our contemporary culture? Why do you think it's important for Paul to work toward securing "undistracted devotion to the Lord"? What can you do in your own life to increase your devotion to God?

3

◊ ◊ ◊

CONTENT IN WHO YOU ARE

The Main Point

A kingdom single lives a life of contentment, which means to be at ease where you are until you get to where you want to be.

The Gathering

To find out more about God's plan of contentment for the single Christian, read the following excerpt from *Kingdom Single*. If you have time, answer the questions that appear at the end of the selection. Or you can finish the section at home.

 ## CONTENTMENT'S GAIN

Perpetual singleness was never a part of God's original intention for most people. The Dominion Covenant is clear that God's purpose for all mankind included male and female marriages that multiplied the human race through childbearing. This, then, resulted in the worldwide expansion of His kingdom agenda (Genesis 1:26-28).

However, when sin entered the human race, with it came selfishness, abuse, immorality, abandonment, divorce, desertion, and death. All these things and more contribute to an overabundance of singleness. This reality has caused even committed Christian singles to have to live a portion or all their lives with unfulfilled desires, dreams, and passions. The fact that a single is saved does not automatically cancel or override the physical, emotional, and relational desires common to humanity.

What, then, is God's means for addressing this reality? The answer is God's grace gift of contentment. While contentment does not cancel the loss that Christian singles experience, it does give them the spiritual capacity to be okay in spite of it.

This is why the apostle Paul could write of simultaneously having lack and yet also contentment. Contentment didn't remove the lack in his life, but it transcended it in such a way that he could successfully handle the unfulfilled areas. Contentment enabled Paul to avoid becoming ensnared in the pull of that which would take him off course for God's best in his life.

A lack of contentment leaves a person open to a wide array of temptations, as well as their resultant consequences. While the single life is often punctuated with gaps and with loss, living it in a spirit of discontent can lead to an even greater degree of loss in many ways.

The story is told of a dog that was wandering around its owner's yard one day. The dog was carrying a large bone in its mouth. When the dog came to the edge of a pond, it looked into the water and saw a reflection of what it thought was an even larger dog with what seemed to be an even larger bone. Wanting the bigger bone, the dog immediately opened its mouth to go after it. Yet in the process, the bone in its mouth dropped into the water and quickly sank to the bottom, out of reach. Not only did the dog fail to get the illusion of the larger bone, but it also lost the one it had been enjoying all along.

Discontent has a way of causing us to lose what we already have in an effort to gain what often does not even exist.

How many Christian singles have given up their well-being, peace of mind, health, hope, and hearts in an effort to go after the illusion of intimacy and wholeness without the bonds of marriage or without entering into the right kind of kingdom marriage? Far too many have done so, based on the flow of tears in my office while counseling single after single for more than four decades now. Far too many wind up with less of themselves while searching for that someone to complete them, failing to realize that they are to be complete in who they are alone. Marriage, then, becomes an added bonus.

Not being satisfied with what you already have is the quickest path to losing it.[1]

Describe contentment in your own words. In what ways does social media influence people's contentment? What are some dangers of living in a spirit of discontent? What happens when we lose focus on what we have in order to seek what we don't have?

Show Time!

In session 3 of the *Kingdom Single Group Video Experience*, Dr. Evans lays out the third principle in our study: Contentment is key for kingdom singles.

◊ ◊ ◊

After viewing Tony Evans' presentation "Content in Who You Are," use the following questions to help you think through what you saw and heard.

1. Dr. Evans begins his talk by stating that being content doesn't mean you won't want:

   ❏ a better job
   ❏ a larger income
   ❏ to get married someday
   ❏ to have children, or have more children

   Check the items above that you would like to have.

Now, take a moment to list other items you are hoping for that are more specific to you:

- ☐ _____
- ☐ _____
- ☐ _____
- ☐ _____

2. Dr. Evans said that contentment doesn't mean you stop dreaming. But contentment does mean that you're not living a worried life while you wait.

   How can you apply this concept to the items you checked or listed above?

3. We can become discontented even during times of great blessing. Describe the blessings Eve enjoyed in the Garden of Eden.

Dr. Evans explained that Eve sinned because Satan created discontentment in her heart. Describe Eve's discontentment.

In what ways did Eve sin? What did she lose as a result of her sin?

What might we lose when we give in to discontentment?

How does a lack of contentment keep Christian singles from fully engaging their time, talents, and treasures for the purposes of God?

4. Which of the following areas have caused you to feel discontented as a single? Check the boxes of the ones that apply or write in your own.

- ☐ seeing other married couples in person or on social media
- ☐ watching romantic movies or shows such as dating reality shows
- ☐ carrying a large load alone (work, house chores, kids)
- ☐ attending church events or classes that cater to couples
- ☐ interacting with people asking you when you are going to get married
- ☐ seeking your own "ideal" of marriage
- ☐ engaging in conversations about marriage or spouses
- ☐ other _____
- ☐ other _____
- ☐ other _____

For every item you checked, list one thing you can be grateful for related to that item. For example, if you checked the first box, then you might write: "I'm grateful to You, Lord, that these images and posts on social media provide me with something tangible to look forward to." Do this for each item you checked.

5. How can you be more intentional about thanking God
rather than complaining?

Read the following Scripture passages, and write down
one thing from each verse for which you are thankful.

Psalm 136:26

Isaiah 41:10

Zephaniah 3:17

1 Corinthians 15:57

6. Dr. Evans taught that contentment is not automatic: It must be learned. What are some things God may do to help you learn this valuable lesson?

How has God used your past experiences to teach you to be content? If you feel led to do so, share this with others.

7. Read about Paul's thorn in the flesh in 2 Corinthians 12:7-10. Why did God choose not to remove the thorn?

How did this help Paul learn contentment?

When God answers our prayers, He may say yes, no, or wait. How do all of these answers teach us contentment?

8. Dr. Evans said that contentment is when God is stabilizing you—when the circumstances are not in your favor, and you have to lean on Him in a way you wouldn't normally have to lean on Him.

   What lessons can we learn by leaning fully on God in situations where we have little or no ability to help ourselves?

9. How will you know when God has shown up in your circumstances or need? Check the one that always applies. God will:

   ____ change the situation into what you wanted and prayed for.

   ____ give you new strength to face the situation well.

10.Read the following excerpt from *Kingdom Single* and reflect
on the questions at the end.

 ## LETTING GO

Contentment must be learned, and that will require going through some
experiences you may not want to go through. God teaches us contentment
by allowing or creating changes in our circumstances, even (or especially)
when those changes are not positive, and then instructing us through the
outcomes of our responses, whether negative or positive.

The definition of contentment is to be at ease and satisfied regardless
of what's happening around you or to you. As a single, that means living
in a spirit of contentment even without the romantic partner you may
long for. Or it could mean allowing your dating relationship to develop
over an extended period rather than rushing to a level well beyond what
singleness calls for. It also may mean letting go of that person you need
to let go of. As my daughter Chrystal says, "Sometimes you have to let
go of what's killing you, even if it's killing you to let go." Contentment
gives you the emotional stability and security to walk away from a toxic
relationship without regret.

As long as your emotional well-being is tied to your circumstances
or to another person (or lack thereof), it remains temporary. Emotions
can go up, down, and all around like a roller coaster because you haven't

learned not to allow the situation, conversation, or relationship to dictate your ease, sense of satisfaction, happiness, and peace.

What constant and even drastic circumstantial changes in our lives, work, and relationships cause us to do (if we allow them to teach us) is to take our eyes off the changing seasons and place our focus instead on the unchanging Lord. Through this, we can learn the art of distancing our emotional well-being from our circumstances and other people. When you discover how to do this through practice, you will also discover how to make life choices from a position of strength rather than one of need.[2]

Dr. Evans referred to his daughter Chrystal Evans Hurst's statement: "Sometimes you have to let go of what's killing you, even if it's killing you to let go." Explain this principle in your own words. What situations in your life is God using to teach you contentment? Pray about this now.

Transformation Moments

Read the following passage from the book of Matthew. Answer the questions that follow. If you run out of time, finish this section at home.

For this reason I say to you, do not be worried about your life, as to what you will eat or what you will drink; nor for your body, as to what you will put on. Is not life more than food, and the body more than clothing? Look at the birds of the air, that they do not sow, nor reap nor gather into barns, and yet your heavenly Father feeds them. Are you not worth much more than they? And who of you by being worried can add a single hour to his life? And why are you worried about clothing? Observe how the lilies of the field grow; they do not toil nor do they spin, yet I say to you that not even Solomon in all his glory clothed himself like one of these. But if God so clothes the grass of the field, which is alive today and tomorrow is thrown into the furnace, will He not much more clothe you? You of little faith! Do not worry then, saying, "What will we eat?" or "What will we drink?" or "What will we wear for clothing?" For the Gentiles eagerly seek all these things; for your heavenly Father knows that you need all these things. But seek first His kingdom and His righteousness, and all these things will be added to you.

So do not worry about tomorrow; for tomorrow will care for itself. Each day has enough trouble of its own.

MATTHEW 6:25-34

Most of us do not worry about what we will eat or what we will wear. However, these were common worries for many people when Christ spoke these words. What are some common worries that singles have today? Does God care about the things you listed as much as He cares about food and clothing? Why or why not? What does it mean to "seek first His kingdom and His righteousness"? Give practical examples. List three things you can do this week to reduce your worry and increase your pursuit of contentment in Christ.

4

◊ ◊ ◊

CLAIMING YOUR ENTIRE VICTORY

The Main Point

As a kingdom single, your victory has already been declared in Jesus Christ, but there are still battles to be fought and struggles to overcome.

The Gathering

To find out more about how to overcome the pull of the flesh and live by the Spirit, read the following excerpt from *Kingdom Single*. If you have time, answer the questions that appear at the end of the selection. Or you can finish the section at home.

 ## THE STRUGGLE IS REAL

Struggles can come in all shapes and sizes. It could be an addiction to pornography or gambling. It could be codependency. It might be an emotional affair with a married person. It could be a propensity toward promiscuity, alcohol, too much spending, or any number of things. Struggles and crises lead us into addictions and challenges that are often difficult to overcome. So whatever your greatest struggle is, as we look at how Paul faced his own, insert yours into the equation, because what he has to say applies to you and how you can overcome the pull of the flesh and live victoriously in the Spirit.

In Romans 7, Paul lays out his struggle in a number of verses:

> For we know that the Law is spiritual, but I am of flesh, sold into bondage to sin. (Romans 7:14)

> For what I am doing, I do not understand; for I am not practicing what I would like to do, but I am doing the very thing I hate. (Romans 7:15)

> So now, no longer am I the one doing it, but sin which dwells in me. (Romans 7:17)

> But if I am doing the very thing I do not want, I am no longer the one doing it, but sin which dwells in me. (Romans 7:20)

Through these verses and more, Paul is being authentic and vulnerable in explaining his battle with his flesh and temptations. While he (and we) received a new nature, our sinful flesh still battles to please itself. The flesh is that unredeemed humanity we all have that seeks to satisfy itself independently of God. Men, the fact that Paul had to battle and find spiritual victory over his flesh as a single man ought to encourage you to do the same. Single men, like the apostle Paul, must work to "discipline my body and make it my slave" (1 Corinthians 9:27).

If you don't discipline your flesh, your flesh will rule. What's worse, Paul tells us that the flesh actually feeds off the law. In Romans 7:11 he says, "For sin, taking an opportunity through the commandment, deceived me and through it killed me." Essentially, the Old Testament Mosaic law actually provoked a greater desire to break the commandments than to keep them. And while Paul desired in his spirit to obey God, he desired in his flesh to disobey God. Sound familiar? It's a schizophrenic kind of crisis that everyone faces at some point, if not in many points in life. It's the battle of the flesh.[1]

What are some common struggles and temptations that singles may face more than other groups? In what ways does our culture contribute to these struggles? How does focusing on ways to overcome a temptation actually increase your thoughts about it and possibly contribute to worsening its grip on you?

Show Time!

In session 4 of the *Kingdom Single Group Video Experience*,
Dr. Evans lays out the fourth principle in our study: Supernatural
power will override natural tendencies when you walk in the Spirit.

◊ ◊ ◊

After viewing Tony Evans' presentation "Claiming Your Entire
Victory," use the following questions to help you think through
what you saw and heard.

1. Dr. Evans states that our victory is secured in Christ: It has
   already been won. What does he mean by this?

2. Despite this certain victory, Christians still struggle
   with sin. Dr. Evans described the battle of the flesh
   that Christians fight. Describe that battle in your own
   words.

Why is the battle of the flesh so difficult? Do all Christians fight this battle? Explain your answer.

Read Romans 7:14-15, 20: "For we know that the Law is spiritual, but I am of flesh, sold into bondage to sin. For what I am doing, I do not understand; for I am not practicing what I would like to do, but I am doing the very thing I hate. . . . But if I am doing the very thing I do not want, I am no longer the one doing it, but sin which dwells in me." According to Paul, what caused his stumbling and sins?

3. How do kingdom singles use "spiritual Spanx" to deal with sin in their lives?

Check the boxes of the things singles may want to cover up with "spiritual Spanx" and list your own.

- ☐ jealousy
- ☐ immorality
- ☐ addictive behaviors, whether binge-watching or excessive social media
- ☐ discontent
- ☐ unforgiveness
- ☐ pride
- ☐ need to control
- ☐ other _____
- ☐ other _____
- ☐ other _____

Dr. Evans says that trying to make the flesh spiritual is "sin management." Why is it impossible to adequately manage the flesh?

4. Many Christians live with a mind-set of shame and guilt because they can't manage their flesh. What negative

consequences can that mind-set produce in our thoughts, words, and actions?

Read Romans 8:1-2: "Therefore there is now no condemnation for those who are in Christ Jesus. For the law of the Spirit of life in Christ Jesus has set you free from the law of sin and of death." Why is it so critical to know that as a Christian you aren't condemned for your sins?

5. What is the solution to overcoming the flesh and the sinful struggles we face as believers? (Refer to Romans 7:25.)

Dr. Tony Evans compared the two laws in Romans 8:2 to gravity and aerodynamics. How does one law overrule the other?

6. How can Christians activate the law of the Spirit? (Refer to Galatians 5:16-18.)

   What does it mean to walk by the Spirit?

7. Scripture promises that if we walk by the Spirit, we won't fulfill the desires of the flesh. However, Dr. Evans reminds us that this doesn't mean we won't feel those desires. Why do you think God allows us to experience temptation rather than taking it away?

   Identify a personal struggle you would like to overcome. You don't have to write it down. Ask God to infuse you with His Spirit and enable you to walk more closely with Him through studying His Word and through worship.

8. Read the following excerpt from *Kingdom Single* and reflect on the questions at the end.

 SET YOUR MIND ON THE SPIRIT

Your victory and your peace come from where you choose to set your mind. They depend on where you decide to allow your thoughts to go. They depend on what you allow into your mind by way of entertainment, music, and conversation. They depend on whether you make time to meditate on God's Word and His attributes and your personal life decisions. They depend on whether you rebuke and cast down thoughts that are contrary to God's truth. The mind set on the Spirit, which is God's way of thinking on a matter, is your key to victory as a kingdom single.

It is unfortunate today that many Christian singles are simply out of their minds. By that I mean that their minds are not functioning rightly. They're living with an improper or distorted mind-set and then wondering why their souls aren't working well and why they're struggling so much. But the answer to that is simple, because the mind is to the soul what the brain is to the body—the centerpiece of function.

If a person's brain fails to operate as it should, that person's body will reflect it immediately. There's simply no way around the cause-and-effect connection of the brain to the body. Similarly, when our minds get off track from a kingdom-based mind-set, our choices, thoughts, and ultimately our souls suffer the consequences. If you have a messed-up, carnal mind, you'll have a messed-up soul. And if you have a messed-up soul, you'll have a messed-up body, because your body functions based on the dictates of your soul.

Since the mind is the key with which you unlock data for the soul, how your mind is oriented and how it not only interfaces with but also filters and applies that data will determine your well-being and progress as a kingdom single.

In the book of Colossians, Paul gives us clear and explicit insight into where and how our minds are to operate as believers in Christ. We read,

> Therefore if you have been raised up with Christ, keep seeking the things above, where Christ is, seated at the right hand of God. Set your mind on the things above, not on the things that are on earth. (Colossians 3:1-2)

In this passage, Paul instructs us that we are to adopt a mind-set that stems from where Jesus is located. We are to seek things above with Christ, but also from the vantage point of Christ, who is seated at the right hand of God the Father.[2]

In contemporary culture, what earthly things do we set our minds on? How do these things keep us from setting our minds on the things of God? What are some practical ways you can refocus your attention daily on God's Word?

Transformation Moments

Read the following passage from the book of Colossians. Answer the questions that follow. If you run out of time, finish this section at home.

Therefore if you have been raised up with Christ, keep seeking the things above, where Christ is, seated at the right hand of God. Set your mind on the things above, not on the things that are on earth. For you have died and your life is hidden with Christ in God. When Christ, who is our life, is revealed, then you also will be revealed with Him in glory.

Therefore consider the members of your earthly body as dead to immorality, impurity, passion, evil desire, and greed, which amounts to idolatry. For it is because of these things that the wrath of God will come upon the sons of disobedience, and in them you also once walked, when you were living in them. But now you also, put them all aside: anger, wrath, malice, slander, and abusive speech from your mouth. Do not lie to one another, since you laid aside the old self with its evil practices, and have put on the new self who is being renewed to a true knowledge according to the image of the One who created him—a renewal in which there is no distinction between Greek and Jew, circumcised and uncircumcised, barbarian, Scythian, slave and freeman, but Christ is all, and in all.

So, as those who have been chosen of God, holy and beloved, put on a heart of compassion, kindness, humility, gentleness and patience; bearing with one another, and forgiving each other, whoever has a complaint against anyone; just as the Lord forgave you, so also should you. Beyond all these things put on love, which is the perfect bond of unity. Let the peace of Christ rule in your hearts, to which indeed you were called in one body; and be thankful. Let the word of Christ richly dwell within you, with all wisdom teaching and admonishing one another with psalms and hymns and spiritual songs, singing with thankfulness in your hearts to God. Whatever you do in word or deed, do all in the name of the Lord Jesus, giving thanks through Him to God the Father.

COLOSSIANS 3:1-17

In what practical, tangible ways can a person seek "the things above"?

Paul includes "anger, wrath, malice, slander, and abusive speech" in the list of things we are to set aside. What are some things we should set aside that relate specifically to being single?

When we are told to let Christ's peace rule, it isn't optional. To resist is to be disobedient to God. Give an example of one way you could allow Christ's peace to rule in your heart, as it relates to any of your struggles as a single.

Paul instructs us twice in this passage to give thanks. In what ways does gratitude contribute to living victoriously over temptations and struggles?

5

◊ ◊ ◊

CAPITALIZING ON YOUR AUTHORITY

The Main Point

As a kingdom single, you've been endowed with authority. Your spiritual authority allows you to have command over your realm of influence, but it comes with a condition: forgiveness.

The Gathering

To find out more about spiritual authority, read the following excerpt from *Kingdom Single*. If you have time, answer the questions that appear at the end of the selection. Or you can finish the section at home.

 ### STUCK OR SUCCESSFUL?

[Many singles have] heard all this good stuff about Jesus. They've heard about a peace that passes understanding. They've heard that the joy of the

Lord is our strength, and that He has come to give life and give it more abundantly. And yet this beautiful thing called Christianity just doesn't seem to be much fun. Fully and freely enjoying your life as a kingdom single, when outside stuff is ruining your outlook and internal emotions are bringing you down, seems to leave a person empty, helpless, and in a passive state of mind.

In fact, far too many singles are living in a cycle of perpetual defeat—never able to overcome, simply subject to life's circumstances. In this manner, a feeling of helplessness to do anything about the mess and misery smothers hope. It creates a life of endurance rather than a life of exploration, where just getting through the day becomes an accomplishment in itself.

Truth be told, many singles are unhappy Christians who believe the right stuff but are finding that it just doesn't work when it comes to them. They say "amen" to the right things, affirm the right doctrines, yet locating the greatness of God that they talk and sing about looms out of reach. One reason this reality rings true for so many singles is that there's a disconnect between the spiritual authority that belongs to every believer and the actual accessing of that authority.

The concepts of singleness and authority don't tend to naturally pair up. Our culture has trained us into recognizing the power of a group. Being single can often lead to feelings of loneliness, isolation, and even inadequacy. These are not accurate definitions of singleness, but they are common, recurring associations with it. The concept of a *strong single* rarely comes up. Rather, we hear about the *struggling single* or the *waiting single* or the *stuck single*, as if being single lacks an essential component necessary for a full life. Because of this, owning and exercising spiritual authority may seem like a foreign concept altogether.

You may be surprised to discover, however, that singles have a unique opportunity to live a life of spiritual authority. This is because of the freedom found in individual stewardship. Whether that freedom involves a greater opportunity to focus, to develop yourself, or even to take risks of faith, singleness positions each person for a wonderful season of spiritual depth and authority.[1]

In what ways do you see Christian singles "living in a cycle of perpetual defeat" or living a "life of endurance rather than a life of exploration"? Tony Evans mentioned the "stuck single," the "struggling single," and the "waiting single." List concepts God would attach to singles based on His Word and His view of singles. What are some opportunities single people have for individual stewardship that married people don't have?

Show Time!

In session 5 of the *Kingdom Single Group Video Experience*, Dr. Evans lays out the fifth principle in our study, which is the principle of personal spiritual authority.

After viewing Tony Evans' presentation "Capitalizing on Your Authority," use the following questions to help you think through what you saw and heard.

1. Read the biblical account of the withered fig tree from Mark 11:12-14, 20-26. What do you think the disciples were thinking and feeling when they saw the withered tree?

What was Jesus' reply to Peter?

What does the mountain represent?

What does this biblical account teach about faith, prayer, and authority?

2. Dr. Evans clarifies that while we are to have faith in God, we are to talk to the mountain. What does it look like in day-to-day life to talk to the problem or issue you are facing? What words would you use when talking to it?

How is this different from our normal response to difficult situations?

Take a moment to practice speaking to any issue of yours that comes to mind. Align your words to Christ's truth as revealed in Scripture. Then speak with authority.

3. What does Jesus say about forgiveness in Mark 11:25-26?

Why does Jesus include this teaching?

4. Dr. Evans explains two types of forgiveness—unilateral and transactional. Describe both in your own words and explain why each is a challenge to live out.

Unilateral:

Transactional:

5. Read Romans 12:19: "Never take your own revenge, beloved, but leave room for the wrath of God, for it is

written, 'Vengeance is Mine, I will repay,' says the Lord."
How does this verse encourage us to more easily forgive?

If you're carrying unforgiveness toward someone, you
are preventing your own progress in life. Is holding a
grudge worth hurting yourself? Why or why not?

In what other ways can forgiveness empower you to live
a life of authority?

6. Dr. Evans shared how God used the sins of others to
   prepare Nelson Mandela to lead a nation. Name a biblical
   example where God used negative circumstances to prepare
   someone to fulfill His purpose.

Based on this example, how can forgiving others give you a greater opportunity to live out your personal calling?

7. Think of someone you need to forgive. Ask God to empower you to forgive. Write down any thoughts or Scriptures the Lord gives you during your prayer time.

8. Read the following excerpt from *Kingdom Single* and reflect on the questions at the end.

MOVING MOUNTAINS AND
CHANGING HEARTS

Moving mountains by faith doesn't take a ton of faith. In fact, a little dab will do you. What it does take is the placement of that faith in the one and only God who can move those mountains. Thus, the reason you need to know God well is that you need to know His character, His Word, and His promises. You need to know what you can honestly expect from Him, because if you don't know what you can expect from Him, you may be believing Him for something you should not be believing Him for, because His Word and character never said He'd provide it. Only as there is legitimate faith in God do you get to exercise legitimate command on earth. If you have illegitimate faith in God because you have misunderstood, misinterpreted, or failed to know His promises, you cannot exercise authority.

Yet when you have faith in the veracity of the God of the Bible, you can simply command whatever mountain you are facing in your life to move, and it will move. Jesus said in [Mark 11:24], "Therefore I say to you, all things for which you pray and ask, believe that you have received them, and they will be granted you." Now, any grammarian or copy editor may have taken a red pen to that passage. After all, it contains three different tenses:

Present tense: All things for which you pray and ask, believe

Present perfect tense: that you have received them,

Future tense: and they will be granted you.

This present-, present perfect-, and future-tense reality of faith and prayer is something we often overlook. But it holds the key to accessing your spiritual authority.

Let me ask you a question: When you believe you "have received" something, how does that affect your emotions, actions, and thoughts? For example, if you ordered a hamburger at a drive-through window, how would believing that the reception of that hamburger was a "done deal" impact your actions? If you doubted, would you drive up to the next window, or possibly pull away? Would you pay ahead of time, or be hesitant to pay at all? Would you start salivating on the way to the second window, or still focus on the hunger pangs gnawing inside you?

Believing that something is a "done deal" affects everything. That's faith.

Putting it in the context of singleness, if you pray for a godly mate and that God will introduce you to him or her, and if you believe this answer is a "done deal" based on God's Word, do you still need to go to the club? Do you still need to worry about the clock ticking away? Do you give yourself away sexually to someone you're just dating? Or are you more apt to move forward in your life—do things like repair your credit score, remove your debt, get physically fit, mentally plan your honeymoon, take those extra classes to finish your master's degree, and more—if you know this is a "done deal"?[2]

Describe the difference between legitimate faith and fake faith. How does authentic faith affect your emotions as well as how you use your time? What would change in your life, thoughts, and conversations if you knew beyond a shadow of a doubt that your faith could move the mountains that you face in your life?

Transformation Moments

Read the following passage from the book of Mark. Answer the questions that follow. If you run out of time, finish this section at home.

As they were passing by in the morning, they saw the fig tree withered from the roots up. Being reminded, Peter said to Him, "Rabbi, look, the fig tree which You cursed has withered." And Jesus answered saying to them, "Have faith in God. Truly I say to you, whoever says to this mountain, 'Be taken up and cast into the sea,' and does not doubt in his heart, but believes that what he says is going to happen, it will be granted him. Therefore I say to you, all things for which you pray and ask, believe that you have received them, and they will be granted you. Whenever you stand praying, forgive, if you have anything against anyone, so that your Father who is in heaven will also forgive you your transgressions. [But if you do not forgive, neither will your Father who is in heaven forgive your transgressions."]

MARK 11:20-26

Why is it often so difficult to truly forgive? How can you know when you have truly forgiven? Consider other situations in your life where you need to forgive someone. Ask God to help you authentically forgive, be set free, and begin to operate with full authority. You may want to write a letter to someone you need to forgive.

6

◊ ◊ ◊

CALLING ON GOD WITH POWER

The Main Point

You won't see what God plans to do in your life until you combine calling on Him with your obedience to Him. Obedience precedes divine movement, especially when God wants to do something special.

The Gathering

To find out more about calling on God, read the following excerpt from *Kingdom Single*. If you have time, answer the questions that appear at the end of the selection. Or you can finish the section at home.

 ### TIME FOR A RESURRECTION

Perhaps you feel it's not fair that you're unmarried or that your mate walked out on you; maybe you lost your mate and now you're a widow or widower. Perhaps you feel your job situation isn't fair or your finances are wrong, and you just want to throw the red flag out on God. Your life is not where you want it to be. Despite all your best efforts at keeping a positive outlook, your chin up, and your feet moving forward, at the end of the day—when it's just you sitting there alone—you believe that God has made a bad call along the way. . . .

Just as God raised Lazarus from his grave, so also God can raise up people today from their sense of loss and bring them back to life as kingdom men and women. Single reader, God has a plan that includes both the ordinary and extraordinary things in life. But His plan is always timed to His agenda, not yours. However, you can delay His plan if you choose to remain in your disappointment for things that have not gone according to your plans. If Martha or Mary had chosen to argue, sulk, and simply ignore Jesus' request to move the stone, they might have never gotten their brother back.

Don't let this life pass without your discovering God's extraordinary gifts and redemption for you because you choose to remain so disappointed with Him that you skip moving the stones He asks you to move. You will never discover God's secret will until you obey His revealed will.

What is the stone you need to move? Is it a person you need to cut ties with? Is it sexual activity you need to stop participating in? Is it a pursuit of your career or calling with more intentionality and passion? Whatever the stone is, it's your job to move it.

And keep in mind, the task may not make sense from a human

perspective. I understand that when something or someone dies, there's a loss of hope. Things look as if they're over, dead. Some of you have dreams that have died. Others have had a previous marriage or relationship that died. And your hope is gone. But do you know why Jesus hung back and allowed Lazarus to die? He did so in order that those around Him could experience a resurrection through a miracle. The only way you can ever get a resurrection in your life is when something dies first—when it's over, as far as humanity is concerned.

When you consider your present situation and see that the natural world is not offering the solution you desire, could it be that God is delaying because He wants you to see what a resurrection looks like? Never let a stone block your miracle. Never let human wisdom and rationale block your miracle. Never let what your friends think or say block your miracle. Cry out to Jesus and to Him alone. Then, when you hear from Him, do what He says to do. He is the source of your resurrection.[1]

What does it mean to "remain in your disappointment for things that have not gone according to your plans"? Why do so many single Christians lose hope? What does Dr. Evans mean when he asks Christians to move stones? The story about Martha, Mary, Lazarus, and Jesus involves four single people. How does that affect your thoughts on the story, conversations, responses, and connections?

Show Time!

In session 6 of the *Kingdom Single Group Video Experience*, Dr. Evans lays out the final principle in our study: As a kingdom single, your requests and desires must be coupled with obedience to God's revealed will.

◊ ◊ ◊

After viewing Dr. Tony Evans' presentation "Calling on God with Power," use the following questions to help you think through what you saw and heard.

1. Dr. Evans begins with an illustration about the red flag that football coaches throw onto the field to challenge a referee's call. Have you ever wanted to throw a red flag on God? Consider sharing your story.

Why might Martha and Mary have wanted to throw a red flag on Jesus?

2. Jesus delayed for two days before traveling to Martha and Mary. What can you learn from Jesus' delay in reaching Martha and Mary?

How can you apply that lesson to your own situation?

3. Dr. Evans states that God will often delay things because in so doing, He reveals Himself at an even greater level. This then develops your faith so that you can grow in maturity. What other reasons might God have for delaying?

4. When Jesus first arrived, Martha blamed Him for Lazarus' death. Why do you think Jesus didn't respond in anger to Martha for sharing her feelings with Him?

Do you tell God your honest feelings about being single? Why or why not?

How is God honored when we are honest with Him?

5. Martha, Mary, and the others were upset with Jesus for not coming earlier. Yet, when He asked them to roll the stone away, they obeyed Him. In your opinion, why did they obey Jesus?

Is there an area in your life in which God is calling you to greater obedience?

What is holding you back from obeying wholeheartedly?

What risk is there in obeying God? What risk is there in disobeying God?

6. How do you think Martha's thoughts and her faith were different after Jesus rose Lazarus from the dead?

7. Read the following excerpt from *Kingdom Single* and reflect on the questions at the end.

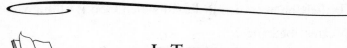

IT THEOLOGY

Sometimes God asks us to let go of something for His sake that we would never let go of other than at a point of crisis. Isn't that what He made Abraham do? He asked Abraham to sacrifice his son—his only son through Sarah, the son whom he loved. When Abraham, in faith, gave his son to the Lord, God gave Abraham back his son.

Luke 6:38 is a powerful verse that we often fail to understand completely, but it directly applies to the fruitfulness and power of our prayers. It says, "Give, and *it* will be given to you. They will pour into your lap a good measure—pressed down, shaken together, and running over. For by your standard of measure *it* will be measured to you in return" (emphasis added).

Notice the word *it* in that verse. That's a small but powerful word. Whatever you're asking God to give you, give *it* to Him. Whatever the substance of your prayers contains that you want God to do for you, change for you, fix for you, or whatever, see how and where the *it* can be given back to God or to others in His name. Hannah wanted a child, so she gave God a child. Abraham wanted his promise of legacy, so he gave God the son through whom that legacy would occur. Give the very *it* that you're seeking, and *it* will be given to you. God is good on His Word.

Are you relationally barren? Then give of yourself relationally to someone else in need, perhaps a shut-in or an elderly person at a group home.

Are you financially struggling? Then by all means be generous to someone else in need—as generous as you can be.

When you step out in faith and give out of your lack to someone else, you're demonstrating that you believe God when, based on your circumstances, believing Him is the last thing you want to do. You're operating on faith even though you can't figure out how and when your solution will ever come.

Do you need answered prayer? Then seek to be the answer to someone else's. The standard of measure you give will be the standard of measure you'll receive in return, and then some. Bear in mind, God usually out-gives us.[2]

How has your own thinking been expanded by studying the purpose of the word *it* in that verse? Can you name someone from the Bible who gave what he or she needed to someone else, only to have it given back? What can you learn from this example? Identify the *it* you are seeking the most, and then look for a way you can meet a similar need in someone else's life while you are waiting on God to meet yours. Write down some options of what you could do.

Transformation Moments

Read the following passage from the book of John. Answer the questions that follow. If you run out of time, finish this section at home.

Therefore, when Mary came where Jesus was, she saw Him, and fell at His feet, saying to Him, "Lord, if You had been here, my brother would not have died." When Jesus therefore saw her weeping, and the Jews who came with her also weeping, He was deeply moved in spirit and was troubled, and said, "Where have you laid him?" They said to Him, "Lord, come and see." Jesus wept. So the Jews were saying, "See how He loved him!" But some of them said, "Could not this man, who opened the eyes of the blind man, have kept this man also from dying?"

So Jesus, again being deeply moved within, came to the tomb. Now it was a cave, and a stone was lying against it. Jesus said, "Remove the stone." Martha, the sister of the deceased, said to Him, "Lord, by this time there will be a stench, for he has been dead four days." Jesus said to her, "Did I not say to you that if you believe, you will see the glory of God?" So they removed the stone. Then Jesus raised His eyes, and said, "Father, I thank You that You have heard Me. I knew that You always hear Me; but because of the people standing around I said it, so that they may believe that You sent Me." When He had said these things, He cried out with a loud voice, "Lazarus, come forth." The man who had died came forth, bound hand

and foot with wrappings, and his face was wrapped around with a cloth. Jesus said to them, "Unbind him, and let him go."

JOHN 11:32-44

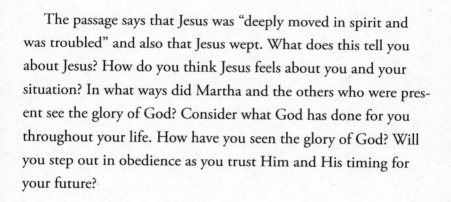

The passage says that Jesus was "deeply moved in spirit and was troubled" and also that Jesus wept. What does this tell you about Jesus? How do you think Jesus feels about you and your situation? In what ways did Martha and the others who were present see the glory of God? Consider what God has done for you throughout your life. How have you seen the glory of God? Will you step out in obedience as you trust Him and His timing for your future?

Acknowledgments

I want to thank my friends at Focus on the Family for their ongoing partnership in bringing my thoughts, study, and words to print. I particularly want to thank Larry Weeden for his critical role in bringing these titles to so many people. I also want to publicly thank Kathy Davis, Liz Duckworth, Marianne Hering, and Beth Robinson.

Working with the video production team at Focus on the Family is always a pleasure as well. Thank you, Blain Andersen, Erin Berriman, Trent Chase, Maurice Diaz, Patrick Dunn, Ross Gunn, John Vencer, and Mitch Wright.

In addition, my appreciation goes out to Heather Hair for her skills and insights in collaboration on this Bible study content and assistance with the video production.

Notes

SESSION 1: COMPLETE AND FULLY FREE
1. Tony Evans, *Kingdom Single* (Carol Stream, IL: Focus on the Family/Tyndale House Publishers, 2018), 9–10.
2. Ibid., 8, 10–13.

SESSION 2: CALLED FOR A PURPOSE
1. Tony Evans, *Kingdom Single* (Carol Stream, IL: Focus on the Family/Tyndale House Publishers, 2018), 30, 32–34.
2. Ibid., 34–35.

SESSION 3: CONTENT IN WHO YOU ARE
1. Tony Evans, *Kingdom Single* (Carol Stream, IL: Focus on the Family/Tyndale House Publishers, 2018), 67–69.
2. Ibid., 75–76.

SESSION 4: CLAIMING YOUR ENTIRE VICTORY
1. Tony Evans, *Kingdom Single* (Carol Stream, IL: Focus on the Family/Tyndale House Publishers, 2018), 90–91.
2. Ibid., 95–96.

SESSION 5: CAPITALIZING ON YOUR AUTHORITY
1. Tony Evans, *Kingdom Single* (Carol Stream, IL: Focus on the Family/Tyndale House Publishers, 2018), 52–53.
2. Ibid., 57–59.

SESSION 6: CALLING ON GOD WITH POWER
1. Tony Evans, *Kingdom Single* (Carol Stream, IL: Focus on the Family/Tyndale House Publishers, 2018), 106–109.
2. Ibid., 118–119.

About Dr. Tony Evans

DR. TONY EVANS is the founder and senior pastor of Oak Cliff Bible Fellowship in Dallas, founder and president of The Urban Alternative, chaplain of the NBA's Dallas Mavericks, and author of more than 100 books, booklets, and Bible studies. The first African American to earn a doctorate of theology from Dallas Theological Seminary, he has been named one of the 12 Most Effective Preachers in the English-Speaking World by Baylor University.

Dr. Evans holds the honor of writing and publishing the first full-Bible commentary and study Bible by an African American.

His radio broadcast, *The Alternative with Dr. Tony Evans*, can be heard on more than 1,300 US outlets daily and in more than 130 countries.

Boundless
Find your place. **Focus your future.**

Join a community

of single young adults

seeking to live kingdom-focused lives.

Visit us at
Boundless.org
A ministry of Focus on the Family

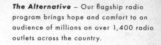